WHEN THE *Glass* BREAKS

KELLEY MORRIS

Raw Earth Ink

2025

For my husband, Gart.
Thank you for making me laugh
and loving me well.
I love you!

This book is a work of poetry.

Copyright 2025 by Kelley Morris

All rights reserved. No part of this book may be reproduced or used in any manner without express written permission from the author except in the case of quotations used in a book review in which a clear link to the source of the quote and its author is required.

First paperback edition March 2025

Interior design by tara caribou

ISBN 978-1-960991-47-8 (paperback)

Published by Raw Earth Ink
PO Box 39332
Ninilchik, AK 99639
www.raw-earth-ink.com

CONTENTS

Living 3
    Glass Houses 4
    Butterflies and Babies 5
    Run Away 6
    Ghosts 7
    Tiny Boxes 8
    To Reach You 9
    Alive 10
    As We Should 11
    Home 12
    Forever 13
    Fine Lines 14
    To Know You 15
    Driving Home 16
    Baby Leaves 17
    The Flower Shop 18
    No Increase 19
Breaking 20
    Shattered 21
    Surrounding Skies 22
    Statistics 23
    Behind Your Smile 24
    Press Rewind 25
    When? 26
    Light and Shadow 27
    Morning News 28
    Raining Tears 30
    What's That Sound 31
    A World Away 32
    Momentary Stops 33
    Grief 34
    Blanket of Rain 35
    Which Came First? 36
    A Little Longer 37
Mending 38
    When The Glass Breaks 39
    Wellspring 40
    Carry Hope 41
    Left Walking 42
    Tug of War 43

The Best Medicine 44
Rebirth 45
Not So Unalike 46
How Are You? 47
In Pieces 48
Quick To Dismiss 49
Both Places 50
Spilling Out 51
A Possibility 52
Colorful Cover 53
Pause and Wonder 54
Reflecting 55
Made of Glass 56
Only One 57
At Seven 58
Such Is The Bond 59
Two Places At Once 60
Connecting The Dots 61
Stillness 62
The Peace of Rain 63
About Wrinkles 64
Good For The Soul 65
Sleeping 66
Cushioned Steps 67
Grandmother Tree 68
No Waiting 69
Childhood Whispers 70
Paint-By-Number 71
About The Author 73

LIVING

A sacred space exists between birth and death, no matter the length of time. It is so much more than time. Influenced by persons, places, and later, choices. Each of us experiences it differently. Whether we embrace it, hide from it, or try and run away from it, life will find us. And sometimes, it just might surprise us.

GLASS HOUSES

What if the
Whole of me
Was on display
Not just one
Tiny window
Showing only
My face to all
Looking in, but
An entire house
Made of glass
Allowing light
Into every crevice
Of my being
Even in the quiet
Corners of my heart
Where only a certain few
Are allowed to look
Would those
Who peer inside
Truly see me for me
Or only the things
I have carefully placed
In the background

BUTTERFLIES AND BABIES

Sweetly swaddled
Snuggled in tight
Outside noises
Muffled
To protect
Tiny ears
Eyes remain
Sheltered
From the
Bright sun
Not yet ready
To greet this world
Until suddenly
Both protected
And protector
Are thrown into
A realm full of
New sounds
New feelings
New sensations
Why should we
Expect anything
Less than tears
And awe
And wonder

RUN AWAY

Bath towel
Pillowcase
Bedsheet
Any material will do
A giant eagle
Flying free
Surveying
The yard
Before perching
On the porch
Superman
Wearing his cape
Ready to swoop in
And save the day
Or maybe
A friendly ghost
Playing a game of
Hide-n-Seek
Shaking with
Silly giggles-
Any material will do
When paired with
The wild imagination
Each child holds
Once they feel free
To let it run away

GHOSTS

Saw ourselves
In both of you
Almost like
Seeing ghosts
A young couple
Starting out
First home
Excited, nervous
Buying used furniture
Our furniture
I could not
Stop smiling
Fought the urge
To wrap you up
In a hug-
Tell you what
An adventure
This life will be
But we don't know each other
Best wishes for your new home!
Hope you enjoy the loveseat!
And you drove off
Ready for your journey
Not really ghosts
But a sweet reminder
Of where our story began
And the chapters
We have written so far...

TINY BOXES

Hours spent
Together
Make me want
To remember
Not just the present
But every visit past-
Each block of time
Long or short
Places another
Tiny box
Inside my heart-
Boxes full
Of surprises
To open when
Days are long
And my mind is
Wandering
Tiny boxes
Fighting battles
Threatening
To take away
Focus, purpose, joy
Tiny boxes
Filled with memories
Of loving and being loved

TO REACH YOU

I'd forgotten
The distance
Required
To reach you
Just one step
And my heart
Quickened
As I heard your voice
Calling thru the trees
Each new step
Taken with purpose
The path becoming
More familiar
Remembering
The distance
Required
To reach you
Answering your song
With every breath
Until finally
The forest cleared
Revealing each drop
Of your roaring cascade
Rushing to the pool
Waiting far below–
And to think,
I almost left
Without visiting

Cedar Falls
Petit Jean Mountain State Park

ALIVE

Sole of my foot
Presses against
Warm concrete
Rocking chair
Gently moves me
Back and forth
As I watch
Pines dance
Across the way
Strong
Graceful
One leaning
Into the next
And the next
Then back again
Their inspiration
Originating
From the same
Cool breeze
Gracing my face-
I am alive
And although
There are no
Instruments
There is no
Melody
There is music
All the same

AS WE SHOULD

Tightly held
Protected
Until time for
The unfurling of
Curved edges
Soft and smooth
Pattern of veins
Barely visible
Vibrant color
Most notable
New and fresh
Like the soft
Smooth skin
Of a newborn
Not yet marked
By time or weather
Though change begins
Immediately
Tossed by winds
Dampened by rains
Warmed by the sun
The steps, incremental
Texture and color
Slowly transforming
The lovely oak leaf
Light to dark greens
Then red or yellow
Finally brown-
Each stage has
Its own beauty
And purpose
Aging, as it should
As we should
Growing
Changing
Transforming

HOME

Today, I heard you
Calling my name
A few notes from
A familiar song
In the passing of minutes
Or maybe seconds
A few notes
But only one word
Each new song the same
One after another
After another
Only a few notes
Still the same word
I heard you again
After the music stopped
This time, I heard a whisper
From the row of pines
Across the road
Their fresh, clean scent
Filling my memories
Their lovely green
Balanced against
The blue sky-
As in the songs
Also, in the pines
I heard you
Calling my name

FOREVER

Such a strange
Thought
Forever
I'm not sure
It can be
Understood
But it's certainly
Beautiful
I haven't seen you in forever!
Spoken with joy
Spoken with regret
Both can fill
The same space
Other times
The word seals
Every hole
In the heart
Despite any lack
Of understanding
Will you marry me?
And this is forever...
Received with security
Received with doubts
Both can fill
The same space-
Thirty years
Of forever, so far
And I still don't
Fully understand
But I am grateful
That forever
Continues to grow

FINE LINES

I sat outside
Long enough
For the sun
To warm my skin
A cool breeze
Made things
A little tricky
Almost keeping me
From discerning
The fine line
Between
Warm or burn
Caused me to compare...
Reminisce or wallow
Sympathize or pity
Love or smother-
One would think
Those simple
To distinguish
And yet,
I've blurred
Their lines
Too many times-
Today, I am grateful
For wisdom felt
In the cool breeze

TO KNOW YOU

Oh, that I would not
Miss the chance
To know you
Past your likes
Past your dislikes
The chance
To offer time
As a gift for us both-
After all, that is
The only way
We truly connect
Occupying
The same space
In the physical
In the technological
Either has the ability
To spark the same magic-
Oh, that I would not
Miss the chance
To know you
Due to the foolishness
Of the words
Too busy-
Is there really such a thing, anyway?

DRIVING HOME

Parallel lines
Well-planned grids
Built to intersect
And connect
It all sounds
So logical
Like tracing a map
With my finger
While my eyes
Follow along-
But one glance
In any direction
And all of the
Straight-line logic
Melts into a sphere
And I am surrounded
By earth and sky
Peace and hope
Past, present, and future
How is it possible?
Sensing the vastness
Of this universe
While driving down
The highway-
I don't know how
But it happened to me
On a Tuesday

BABY LEAVES

All it takes
Is one early
Spring shower
And bright
Green smiles
Suddenly appear
Around every corner
The color is vibrant
So fresh and new
It causes me
To question
Whether or not
It is genuine-
Then, a quiet breeze
Happens to pass
And baby leaves
Begin to wave
Their friendly wave
The smiles growing
Instantly wider
-Theirs and mine-
And I am gently
Reminded to embrace
Each new season
With hope and faith
Oh, and maybe a smile

THE FLOWER SHOP

Perhaps because it was
My thirty-first
Wedding anniversary
Perhaps because your
Silvery white hair
Brought memories of Dad
And the anniversaries
He and Mom celebrated-
I don't know why
I noticed you walking
Into the flower shop
While sitting in
The drive-thru line
Next door, waiting
For my order
Of lemon chicken
But I wondered
Why you were there-
You looked distinguished
In your dark navy slacks
Light blue button-down shirt
And silvery white hair
So many possibilities
For your stop at
The flower shop-
If only I could wait
To see what flowers
You purchased-
But I couldn't wait
There were cars behind
And work ahead-
I picture you and
Your lovely wife
Celebrating your anniversary
Fifty or sixty years, perhaps?
I guess I'll never know
But I'm thankful
My thoughts had
The chance to wander

NO INCREASE

Why are we in such a hurry?
Wishing our days away-
As children
In a hurry
To grow up
As students
In a hurry
To finish first
As young adults
In a hurry
To get married
Start a family-
Realizing our
Foolishness
Right at the moment
We wish for time
To slow down
Our children
To remain little
A bit longer
Our parents
To age
A bit slower
Ourselves
To breathe in
Each moment
Accepting that
Our hurrying
Offers no increase

BREAKING

Within this space called life, there is heartbreak. It cannot be avoided. Of course, circumstances vary greatly from person to person. Sometimes as small as a chip in a favorite coffee mug. Other times, a priceless heart shattered into a million pieces. These experiences may crush us. But they also serve to teach us, if we allow our tears to fall.

SHATTERED

An image destroyed
Countless pieces
Strewn on the ground
A heartbreaking scene
Of loss on display-
Those once interested
In pausing to look
Now quickly turn away
As they murmur
It was probably a fake
Inaccurate representation, at best
It was bound to break
But their murmurings
Are silenced by the one
Who remains close
Carefully picking
Up the pieces
Gently placing them
Back together
Providing restoration
Through the honesty
Of loving hands
And a tender heart

SURROUNDING SKIES

Heaviness lingers in
The quiet struggles
Of others
On this cold
Fall morning-
Though not my own
Fragments
Of their pain
Filter through
My thoughts-
The sky is clear
From my vantage
But white clouds
Of grief and sadness
Fill surrounding skies
Needing to release
Waiting for assurance
That it is ok
For the rain to fall
Even on the clearest of days

STATISTICS

They return every day
Same building
Same rooms
Until some move away
And new ones come
Each one carrying
Their own story
Their own history
Good and bad
Happy and sad
All blended together
Creating empathy
Understanding
Along with conflict
And frustration
But ultimately
Learning that lasts
For a lifetime
And success
Not measurable
By any test
Not represented
By any numbers
They are not statistics
The teachers
Or the students
They are people
Connecting hearts
Healing heartaches
Every day
In this place
We call school

BEHIND YOUR SMILE

Your sweet smile
Gives no hint
Of the hurt
In your heart
They say children are resilient
That may be true
But one heart
Can only hold
So much pain-
When each day
Is framed with loss
And instability
The future will not
Go untouched-
Not to say
There is no hope
Only that there are
No easy answers
Except for the ability
To always return
Your sweet smile

PRESS REWIND

If only it was
Possible
Press rewind
Go back in time
Prevent every
Unkind word
That left you
Confused and alone
Block every
Raised hand
That left you
Hurt and afraid
Unable to defend yourself
From those charged
With your keeping-
But time cannot
Be rewound
Trauma cannot
Be erased
Does time heal all wounds?
I'm afraid some
Are too deep-
If only it was
Possible
Press rewind
Go back in time

WHEN?

Another school day
Filled with laughter
And learning
Shattered by
The sound
Of gunshots
Screams and
Cries for help
Followed by silence-
Children with their teachers
Hiding, frightened
Training put into action
Training that should never
Have been necessary
For actions that should never have occurred

When will we decide enough is enough?
When will we choose love, instead of hate?
When will we weep instead of foolishly
arguing?

Mourning for innocent lives
Left lying on the floor
Of the very place
They should have been safe

LIGHT AND SHADOW

I sat with
The heaviness
All-day-long
My heart wrapped
In a blanket of grief
The day wrapped
In weeping clouds

A peak of the sun
Broke my stillness
Only a glance
Out the window
Surely, I should not soak it in
How could I?
Amid so much suffering

That sweet sunshine
Not to be ignored
Determined to draw me out
Shone a little brighter
Bravely displaying
Light and shadow
Simultaneously

I couldn't help
Whispering
A thank you
Even as my heart
Continued to cry

MORNING NEWS

I sit quietly
In my house
Drinking hot tea
Watching the morning news
Never having experienced
The kind of fear
That would cause me
To flee my home
Searching for a place of safety
A shelter below the ground
Where the explosions above
That will destroy my home
And those of my friends and family
Cannot reach my children-

I don't know that kind of fear
Not fear of natural disasters
Unavoidable depending on location
But fear of weapons
Created by man
Neighbor against neighbor
Strong overtaking weak
Seeking what?
Power and greed seem
The most plausible answers-

I sit quietly
In my house
This morning
Unable to erase the image
Of a precious girl
On the morning news
Her big eyes filled with tears
Hiding underground
Unable to block
The sounds of bombs
Exploding on the surface-

Perhaps I should not try
To erase her image
And instead, let it sear
Into my memory
Reminding me to pray for light
To find her in that dark place

RAINING TEARS

The sky wept
Thru the night
Quieting only
For moments
At a time
To take a quick
Breath of air
That offered
No relief

No lightening
To break
The vast darkness
No thunder
To break
The veil of grief
Only the tears
Of broken hearts
Forever flowing

It must have been raining all over the world

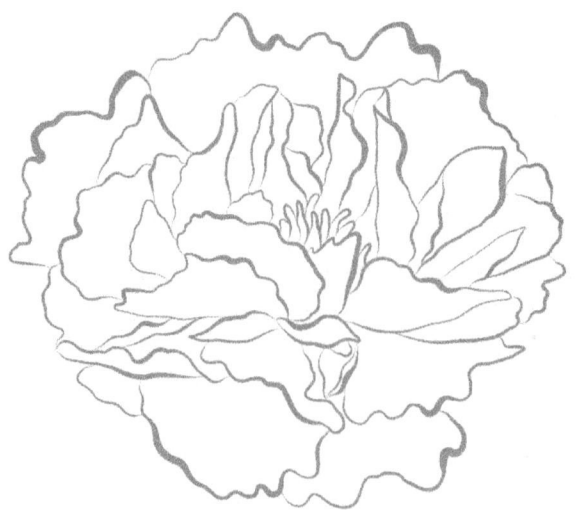

WHAT'S THAT SOUND

I have breathed
The sigh of relief
Heard pure joy
In the laughter
Of my children
Expressed grief
With sounds
Of sobbing
But what about fear?
How does it sound?
The question brings
Only silence
Deliberation halts
My hurried mind
Until heard in the voices of others-
Voices afraid
The next city destroyed
Will be their own
Voices afraid
They may never
See family again
Voices afraid
To hear or even speak
The truth that others
Work to keep hidden forever-
Listen...Do you hear their fears?

A WORLD AWAY

Today feels anything but simple
It feels torn
I feel torn
Sunshine skies
In front of me
Clear and blue
A stark contrast
To images of gray skies
Streets filled with ash
Houses reduced to rubble
Seen on the morning news-
My mind knows
And history tells us
Not all people are free
Or safe from the exploits
Of evil men-Yet my heart
Is unable to reconcile-
An image of another mom
Living a world away
Her only thought
Protecting her family
From the surrounding
Destruction and death...
I cannot know the heaviness of her heart
But I must not look away-
Watching, praying for a glimmer of hope
For a family reunited
While never forgetting the images
Snapped by cameras
Images of death
And innocence stolen
For all the world to see-

MOMENTARY STOPS

Happily sitting
Soaking
In the smiles
An observer
Of the ones
Who make me
What I am
And fill me
To my core
Precious days
Marked by traditions
And Celebration
Momentary stops
On this continuing
Path called
Carrying Grief
Where the hellos
Grow sweeter
And the goodbyes
Last longer-
A temptation
To hold on too tight
Tries to sneak in
But letting go
Through the tears
Is the only way
To feel fresh air
Enter my lungs
Clear my head
And heal my heart

GRIEF

A black cloud
Moved across
The gray
Morning sky
Circling, swirling
Changing shape
Separating
Coming back
Together
Its fluctuations
Matching
My grief-
Moving closer
I could see
It was not
A cloud
But a flock
Of birds-
They landed
On the branches
Of barren trees
Perched up high
Unwavering
Their feathers
A brief replacement
For recently
Fallen leaves
Their stillness
Giving my heart
A moment to rest
To catch my breath
Though tears
Continued to flow

BLANKET OF RAIN

The night sky
Seemed to weep
The weight
Of its tears
Soaking deep
Into the soil
Creating a path
For the colors
Of spring

The night sky
Seemed to sob
The sound
Of its tears
Forming a
Wall of peace
To block
The noise
In my head

The night sky
Seemed to cry
The grace
Of its tears
Replacing mine
If only for
A little while
As peaceful
Sleep returned

WHICH CAME FIRST?

Heaviness weighs
Body and soul
But my brain?
The exact opposite-
I seem to be
In a sort of
Chicken and egg
Scenario
Wondering
Which came first?
Sleeplessness
Sadness
Grief, tears
Spiraling
Anxious
Thoughts-
I suppose
It doesn't matter
Which came first
We are all in this
Together-
My eyes
My body
My brain
My heart
And thankfully, *you*
Right beside me
Reminding me
To breathe
As my tears fall
On your shoulder

A LITTLE LONGER

I seem to be
Spending
More time
Inside my heart
These days
Blocking out
The noisy world
Ignoring my own
Thoughts
So as not
To neglect
A single memory of you-
I know some
Will fade
With time
But for now
It is my heart
That holds
Each image
Your quiet strength
Your gentle smile
Your sky-blue eyes
It is a sacred job
This holding
So, I think
I will remain
Inside my heart
Just a little longer

MENDING

There is no superglue for healing a broken heart. No replacement for a parent, a child, a spouse. No logical explanation for hatred or war. But hope and faith intertwine, offering peace. And the God who loves us, never lets us go. He helps us love each other through sharing both our joy and our sorrow.

WHEN THE GLASS BREAKS

Hairline fracture
Barely visible
Easily repaired
Little lasting effect
At least to those
On the outside
Looking in

A clean break
Additional time
Needed to mend
Leaving behind
An echo of
The original hurt
On cold days

Shattered into
A million pieces
Like blown glass
Dropped on a tile floor
No amount of effort
Able to recreate
The original work of art

The same
May be said
Of broken hearts
Even so, when
Shattered into
A million pieces
Hope is not lost

Examined closely
The sparkle
Left behind
In the shards
Cries out
Ready to be
Made brand new

WELLSPRING

I often forget
The depth of the well
Its capacity to hold
The fluidity of feelings
No matter their origin-
Until one sentiment
Rises to the top
Threatening a flood
Before slowly floating
Down, down, down
Once again resting
At the bottom of the well-
What would happen
If the tide was not
Contained
Allowed to spill over
Soaking its surroundings
With grief, joy, sadness, peace...
Perhaps next time
I feel a catch
In my throat
I'll let my tears fall freely
Then search for my reflection
Along with those of the
Blue sky and green leaves
In the puddle that forms
Beside the tree
Where I choose to rest

CARRY HOPE

Do you ever feel
Restless
Lose track of time
Or your car keys
Focus blurry
From tired body
Tired mind
Too much time
Thinking about
Life's worries-
Place your hands
Over your eyes
As a shield
But remember to
Spread your fingers
Wide enough for
Tiny particles
Of sun dust
To filter thru
The open spaces
And carry hope
Into your heart

LEFT WALKING

Walking
Hand in hand
First day
To last
One often seen
As an enemy
Of the other
Giver vs. Taker-
Picture them
Working
Together
One aiding
The body
Along its path
The other
Waiting to
Embrace the spirit
Once the temporary
Gives out-
Death seen as
A part of life
Not simply
Determiner
Of its end-
Though the ones
That remain
Temporarily walk
With broken hearts
They know it is
A shared journey

TUG OF WAR

Parading around
In costumes
Unfamiliar masks
Distracting me
From the struggle
Taking root
In my soul
Feelings
Can be sneaky
That way
Tricksters thriving
On energy expended
In a tug of war
That leaves me trying
To pull the rope
From both ends-
There will never
Be a winner
Only the need
To let go
Of the rope
Even if it means
Falling in the mud

THE BEST MEDICINE

One would think
The perfect remedy
For curing sadness
Would be listening
To a happy song-
But when feeling low
Who wants to hear
Put on a Happy Face?
Not before wallowing
At least a bit
Though it may sound silly
The best medicine
Just might be
That familiar tune
From a well-worn sad song
I know it doesn't make sense
Treating sadness
With more sadness
But give it a try
Next time you're feeling blue
Let the melancholy notes
Wash over you
Like an old friend
One who sympathizes
One who understands
One who longs
To take your sadness
And add it to their own

REBIRTH

The ground swells
From soaking in
The tears of many
While the sky lowers
From the weight
Of sighs rising
In desperation-
The space in between
Shrinks from the pressure
Creating a fear of
Imminent suffocation
What happens if the two meet?
This groundswell
And lowering sky
I'm not sure they can meet
Other elements are at work-
Kind words
Caring smiles
Acts of courage
Delivering deep breaths
Of fresh air
Drying tears with
A rebirth of hope

NOT SO UNALIKE

If your tears flowed
From my eyes
Would I feel your pain?
Would I understand
What brings you joy?

If my heart
Beat strong
Inside your chest
Would you know my fears?
Sense my excitement?

Physically impossible
And yet if I stare long enough
At your image to gain
A glimpse into your soul
What might be possible?

Would our lives change?
Sympathy morphing
Into understanding
And understanding
Flying into action

I am not you
You are not me
But if we peered deep
Perhaps we would
Grasp the mystery

HOW ARE YOU?

So many ways
To say hello
A smile, a wave
A subtle nod
Even a raised voice
Not due to anger
Simply passing
At a distance
How are you!
Do I really want to know?
Will I slow down and listen?
Walk past or walk closer
Study expression
Notice position
Discern whether
I'm fine
Is an honest answer
Or a cover
For the heart
Desperately
Silently shouting
I could use a friend
Do you have time to talk?

IN PIECES

When tears well up
Let them fall
When your heart aches
Let words flow
When a friend is near
Lean on them
When feeling motionless
Take one step
When tempted to forget
Remember
For that memory
Is a piece of your heart

QUICK TO DISMISS

You and I have
A difference
Of opinion
As far as
Differences
Of opinion go
Since an opinion
Is quite often
Not completely
Based on facts
Perhaps we could
Put this one aside-
Yes, it seems
Important now
Emotions heightened
With every discussion
But is it worth dismissing each other?
Flesh and blood
Heart and soul
Isn't it worth attempting a connection?
If our hands could
Briefly touch
Surely out hearts
Would follow

BOTH PLACES

I'm getting used to
Not knowing
What to expect
Or how to feel
Choosing
Not to view
This turn of events
In a negative light
That would be
A contradiction,
Would it not?
Light has a way of
Lifting, drawing out
Right as the heart
Begins to cry
Whether the tears
Come from the reality
Of grief's reminders
Or from the joy
Of new life's smiles-
Light can live
In both places
Perhaps that lesson
Is teaching me peace
Even in the not knowing

SPILLING OUT

Constantly bombarded
By outside sources
A cunning attempt
To create doubt
Are you happy with your appearance?
Wouldn't you like to be thinner?
Don't you want to look younger?
If those wrinkles
Around my eyes
And in the corners
Of my mouth
Are tracing the years
Of laughter and tears
Why would I erase them?
If my body is
Telling the story
Of birthing three children
Loving the same man
For more than thirty years
And knowing the grief of loss
Why would I not let it speak?
I am a journey
Of experiences
And emotions
Spilling out
Along the road
For others to see
No apologies
Only grace
Accepted
And shared

A POSSIBILITY

Once we became
Acquainted
Hiding was futile
I could either attempt
To ignore you or
Make the best of it
And accept you
For who you are-
The initial shock
Of your rough exterior
Made me want
To runaway
Thankfully, I stayed
Not to say
We are friends
That would be a stretch
But the possibility exists
I sensed it while
Hugging you tight enough
To see into the
Center of your soul
Where sweet memories
Are kept, treasured
So as never
To be forgotten

COLORFUL COVER

Listening to hear
Not simply respond
Speaking to connect
Not simply inform
Linked by
An unseen thread
Of hopefulness-
It can happen
Sitting together
On the couch
During a phone call from
The next state over
Or a chat from
Across the world-
Each new stitch
Creating
A colorful cover
Of understanding-
Your heart beats
Inside your chest
The same as mine
Carefully carrying
Thoughts worth sewing

PAUSE AND WONDER

In the shapes
Of clouds
In the leaves
Of trees
In the feathers
Of backyard birds
It is everywhere
But do we recognize it?
They say...
It is the spice of life.
Maybe there is more to it than that?
In the colors
Of our skin
In the traditions
Of our cultures
In the songs
Of our hearts
Variety draws us in
Gives us cause
To pause
And wonder
Encourages us
To embrace
Our differences
Before showing us
How very much
We are the same

REFLECTING

It begins before we are born. Recognizing voices and sensing movement. Responding to music and stories. A continuous process of growing until we take our last breath. Some lessons may be forced up on us. Others, we choose. Reflecting on our experiences has the power to teach us how to just be.

MADE OF GLASS

If I were made of glass,
What shape would I choose?
A vase for holding flowers
A bowl for sharing soup
A mug for embracing coffee
One that is useful, or
One intended only for display-
The thought of sitting on a shelf
Having contact with
Only the few who
Happen to walk by
And briefly gaze
Has little appeal
Although, it is
The one place flaws
Are easily hidden
If hiding flaws
Serves any purpose-
After some consideration
I think I would prefer
To live in the daylight
Embracing the beauty
Found in each
Reflective imperfection

ONLY ONE

I only get this one body
Beautifully complicated
Strong yet, fragile
An outer shell
Protecting the heart
Beating inside my chest
Brain thinking
Inside my head
Eyes seeing
Outside my world
Bones, muscles, tendons
Connected, carrying me
One step
One thought
One view
At a time-
This one body
That from time to time
Feels pain, frustration,
Inadequacies
From time to time
Experiences the amazing-
Carried three tiny beings
Until they were ready
To meet the world
Wrapped arms around them
Wiped away their tears
Held on to their hands-
Learning to love
This one body
Both its strengths
And weaknesses
This one temporary body
That houses my soul

AT SEVEN

It is difficult
To remember
The me who
Once was seven
Do you find the same to be true?
Oh, there are glimpses
Flashes of childhood
Aided by photographs
And the reciting
Of stories at
Family gatherings-
I believe at seven
Happy outweighed sad
And freedom came
In swinging way up high
High enough to touch the sky
Then bravely jumping out-
It is difficult
To remember
The me who
Once was seven
But I am grateful
For her spirit
Continuing
To reside in me
Even when I'm afraid
To jump out of the swing

SUCH IS THE BOND

There we were
Standing on
Grandma's front porch
Me and Mom
All her sisters
Even Grandma
Was there talking
And smiling

Strange how young
She looked
I should have been
A child-And yet,
There I stood
Seeing them all
Thru grown-up eyes
A gift all its own

As one sister drove away
We all waved thru smiles
And tears, uncertain
When she would return

Such is the bond of
Mothers, daughters, sisters
Pouring love and strength
Thru laughter and tears
Over each new generation
Of mothers, daughters, sisters

I awoke in a sea of emotions
Thankful for the strong women in my past
Thankful for vivid dreams invaded by
memories

TWO PLACES AT ONCE

In certain seasons
Distance
Seems to
Play the role
Of villain
Stealing away
The moments-
If only
I could be
In two places
At the same time
I can't be
In two places
At the same time
At least, not my body
But my heart...
It is here
It is there
Distance
Not really
A villain
Merely life
And me
Wishing the miles
Between us were fewer

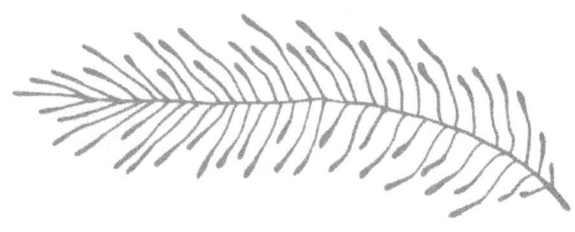

CONNECTING THE DOTS

What if
I created
A map
Dotted with
Colorful pins
String wrapped
Around each pin
Connecting the dots
One to another
Each color holding
Individual meaning
Blue? Content
Orange? Unsure
Green? Happy
Gray? Sad
Except the pins
Wouldn't mark
Places I've travelled
No, this map would be
An outline of my heart
Veins, arteries, valves
Dotted with the
Breath of hearts
Intersecting each
Change of direction

STILLNESS

Unaware
I was searching
Looking up
To the wild sky
Surrounded
By towering pines
Unaware
I was searching
Listening intently
To the bird's morning song
Carried on the afternoon breeze
Unaware
I was searching
Until a stillness
Within the motion
Caught my breath-
There you are!
Aware
I was both
Finder and found

THE PEACE OF RAIN

When clouds
Appear soft
Their colors muted
Blending one
With another
Covering the sky
In a grace-filled
Gentle blanket
Evenly sharing
Their weight
Allowing for
A healing release
Of raindrops so gentle
You barely notice them-
We forgot our umbrella
Should we go back?
Let's follow the raindrops
Into this unexpected reprieve
From the busyness of life

ABOUT WRINKLES

I am choosing
To view wrinkles
In a new light
Especially after
Noticing them
On my eyelids
How does that even happen?
The eyeliner applied resembling
A jagged Jack-O-Lantern smile
Okay, maybe I'm exaggerating
But it did introduce
A new line of questioning
What caused the lines framing my mouth?
Smiling countless smiles
Lines drawn from the corners of my eyes?
Squinting from the brightness of a warm sun
Lines gracing my forehead?
A bit of worry over the ones I love-
All these answers are signs
Traces of living
A life not ready
To be erased
Or to be forgotten

GOOD FOR THE SOUL

Evenly spaced rows
Of gently waving wheat
Wonderfully wound
Bales of hay
Equally sided cubes
Childhood toys
Labeled with letters,
Numbers and pictures
Ready to be
Neatly stacked
Then knocked over
Only to be
Stacked again-
Little hands reaching
Sleepyhead resting
On my shoulder
Comforting weight
Beneath the rise and fall
Of sweet slumber-
Calm exists within
The routine
On any given day-
Whether passing by
Or sitting in the center

SLEEPING

In the quiet
Of the morning
Stoically standing
Seeking no attention
Trees line its ridge
Bare, unmoving
No colors
To catch my eye
And yet, I stop
And stare
As it sleeps-
I imagine its base
Collecting warmth
From the sun's rays
Storing the energy
Soon required for waking
Pushing flowers up
Thru the forest floor
Opening patient buds
On the yawning trees
While crying out
Spring is here!
But today
The mountain sleeps
And I watch
Grateful
For its presence

Pinnacle Mountain State Park

CUSHIONED STEPS

Each careful step
Across the floor
Cushioned by
Layers of history
What was once alive
Now protects as it
Deteriorates
Feeding the earth
Underneath
How many have
Come and gone
Taken these same steps
Across lines of
Time and space-
Did they notice
The Luna moth
Drying her wings
In frilly foliage
Of gentle ferns
Or the bright orange
Mushrooms
Peeking out from
Underneath
The fern leaves
Were their steps cushioned as well?
Steps that allowed
Time for pause
Time for soaking up
All the forest
Has to say
About the past
The present
And the future

GRANDMOTHER TREE

She has lived
Through
Her share of
Heartache
But her beauty
Is what you
Notice first
Standing tall
And refined
Balanced and
Breathtaking
She has lived
Through
Her share of
Heartache
But her arms
Remain raised
Above her heart
Above her head
Reaching past
Her sorrow
Toward the light

NO WAITING

Long drives
Lunches
By the lake
Even on
Rainy days-
Waiting for
Sunny days
Means missed
Moments
The sun
Peeking
From behind
A cloud
To warm
My cold nose
Raindrops
Falling
From above
To cool
My rosy cheeks
Your smile
Reaching
Across the table
To hold my heart

For Mom and Dad

CHILDHOOD WHISPERS

As I walk into
The clearing
Time slowly rewinds
The rises and falls
In this small plot of
Gently rolling land
Are interrupted by
A quiet stream
And perfectly placed oaks
A perimeter of pines
Provides a freedom
Not easily found
In the outside world
Freedom taken for granted
Until life allows for
Both leaving
And returning-
As I walk down
That familiar road
Still shaded by trees
The whispers
Of many childhoods
Are carried on the breeze-
There you are!
We are so glad to see you again.
Won't you come and play?

PAINT-BY-NUMBER

We all begin
As a clean slate
Or do we?
How much of my mom
Was present from
The beginning?
What about my dad?
The physical likenesses
Are obvious, even expected
But what about nature-
Was I already more
Like one than the other?
Or did watching
Their example
Produce gradual growth
Transforming me not
From a blank slate
But from the outline
Of a complex
Paint-by-number portrait
Coming into view
As each new color
Was added and blended
Brushstrokes
Of emotions
And experiences
And connections
Rendering
My journey
Of Becoming

ABOUT THE AUTHOR

Kelley Morris grew up outside Little Rock, Arkansas, a few miles from beautiful Pinnacle Mountain State Park. She has lived most of her adult life in Oklahoma, where she and her husband raised their three children. Kelley is a pianist and former elementary music and special education teacher. She enjoys writing poetry that reflects life and helps her connect with others.

www.ingramcontent.com/pod-product-compliance
Lightning Source LLC
Chambersburg PA
CBHW020020050426
42450CB00005B/566